Hello, my name is Clancy.

About me

My name is _____.

I am in Year _____.

My teacher is _____.

Track your progress

As you complete pages in this book,
trace over the matching letter here.

t

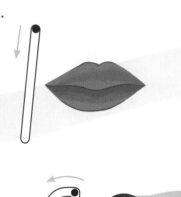

l

a

i

c

e

o

s

z

x 6

as in " six "

GREAT WORK!

Yeah!

j

g

q

OXFORD UNIVERSITY PRESS

Before you begin writing ...

Here are the **3Ps** that will help you with your writing: **p**osture, **p**encil grip and **p**aper position. You will be reminded about these as you work through the book.

Posture

- Relax your arms.
- Sit back in your chair.
- Make sure your back is straight.
- Put your feet flat on the floor.

Pencil grip

Hold your pencil like this. (Not too tightly!)

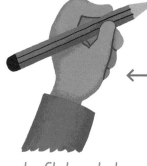

Left-handed

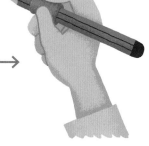

Right-handed

Paper position

Use your non-writing hand to steady the paper.

Left-handed

Right-handed

Hand and finger warm-ups

Crocodile snaps (whole arms)

Start with one arm straight above the head and the other extended down one side of the body. Snap the hands together, like a crocodile snapping its jaws. Repeat, but reverse the arms.

Open, shut them. (hands)

Open, shut them. Open, shut them.
Give a little clap!
Open, shut them. Open, shut them.
Lay them in your lap.
Repeat.

Spider push-ups (fingers)

Place the fingertips together and bend and straighten the fingers while pushing the fingertips against each other.

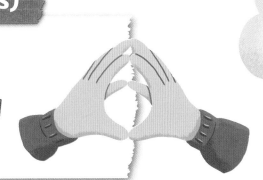

Trace the patterns.

OXFORD UNIVERSITY PRESS

Trace and then continue each pattern.

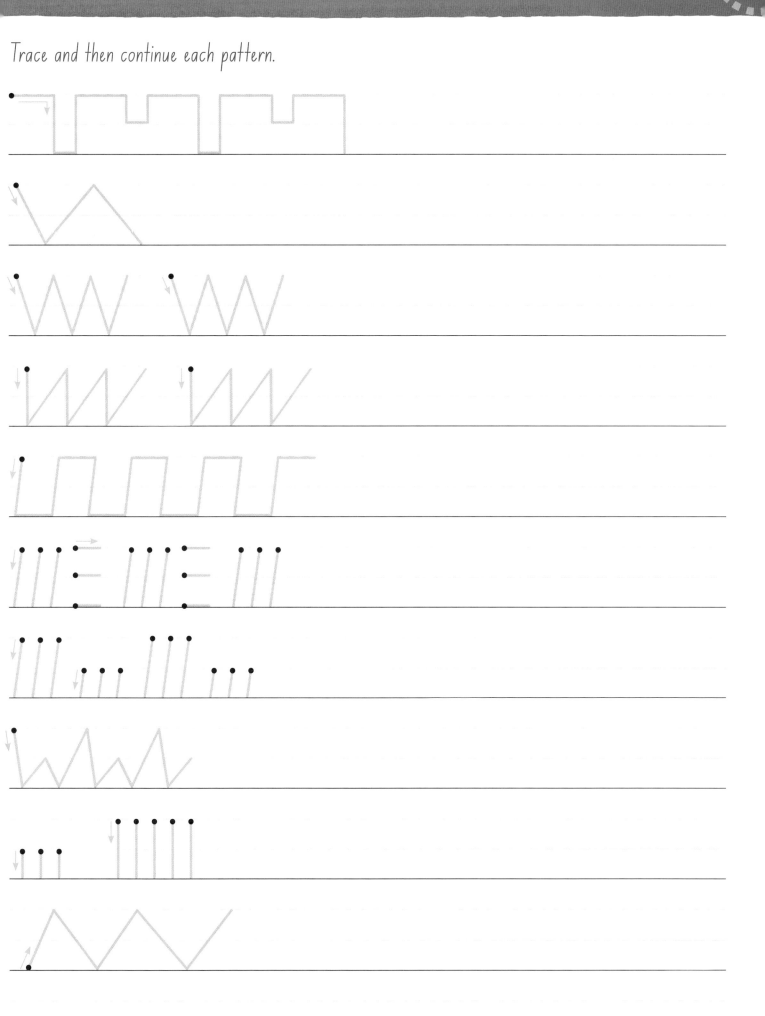

Warm-up patterns for tall letters

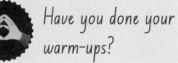

3Ps Have you checked your posture, pencil grip and paper position?

Have you done your warm-ups?

lips

Trace and then copy the letters and words.

live   lives   lived

live

love   loves   loved

love

like   likes   liked

like

l o t i f i d a h

above
on
below

L L L L L L L L L L

L

Lia lives in Alice Springs with

Lia

her family and Lila the lizard.

lizard

Choose some interesting words from the previous page and write them on the lines below.

Tall letter group

above

on

below

3Ps Have you checked your posture, pencil grip and paper position?

Have you done your warm-ups?

treasure

Trace and then copy the letters and words.

take   takes   taking

take

think   thinks   thinking

think

today   tomorrow   yesterday

today

t i f i d a h i b o k

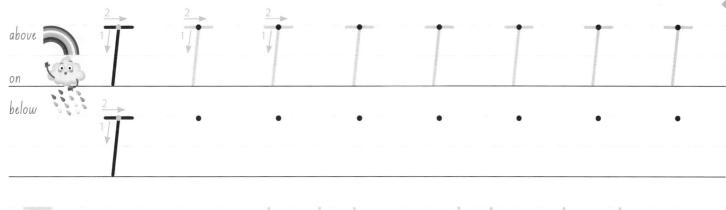

above

on

below

Tam is excited to celebrate his

Tam

tenth birthday today!

tenth

Choose some interesting words from the previous page and write them on the lines below.

Self-assessment Put a circle around your best letter and word on each page. Explain your choice to your teacher or classmate.

3Ps Have you checked your posture, pencil grip and paper position?

Have you done your warm-ups?

floaty

Trace and then copy the letters and words.

f f f f f f f f f f

f

float   floats   floating

float

fly   flying   flew

fly

friend   friends   friendly

friend

f i d a h i b a k o l

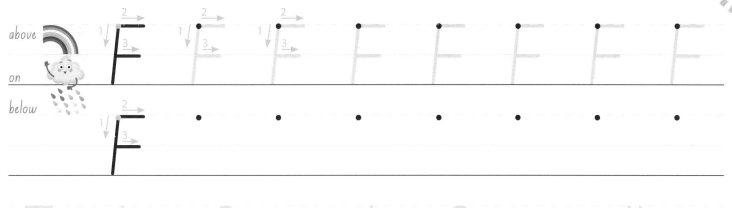

on

below

F F F F F F F F

F

Faz has fun on his fancy yellow

Faz

floaty. His dad watches him.

floaty.

Choose some interesting words from the previous page and write them on the lines below.

Self-assessment Put a circle around your best letter and word on each page.
Explain your choice to your teacher or classmate.

above
on
below

Have you checked your posture, pencil grip and paper position?

Have you done your warm-ups?

helicopter

Trace and then copy the letters and words.

h h h h h h h h h h

h

help   helping   helped

help

heap   heaps   heaped

heap

happy   happiest   happily

happy

h i b a k e l i t o f

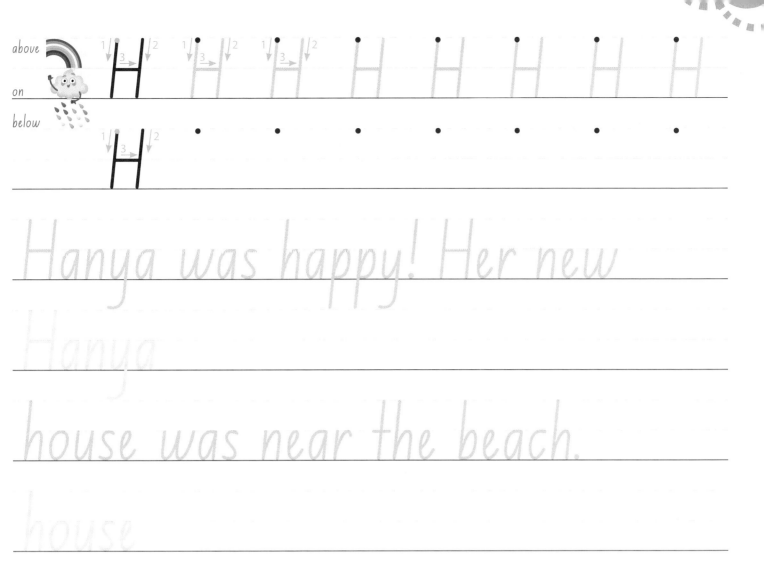

above

on

below

Hanya was happy! Her new

Hanya

house was near the beach.

house

Choose some interesting words from the previous page and write them on the lines below.

above
on
below

3Ps Have you checked your posture, pencil grip and paper position?

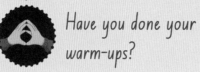
Have you done your warm-ups?

drums

Trace and then copy the letters and words.

d   d   d   d   d   d   d   d   d   d

d   .   .   .   .

dry   dries   drying

dry

did   did not   didn't

did

dislike   dislikes   disliked

dislike

d   e   h   i   b   a   k   o   l   i   t

OXFORD UNIVERSITY PRESS

above

on

below

D D D D D D D D D D D

D

Dusty the dog was the dirtiest

Dusty

that he had ever been!

that

Choose some interesting words from the previous page and write them on the lines below.

3Ps Have you checked your posture, pencil grip and paper position?

Have you done your warm-ups?

bird

Trace and then copy the letters and words.

b b b b b b b b b b

b

big   bigger   biggest

big

break   breaks   breaking

break

behind   below   before

behind

b a k o l i t o f i d

above

on

below

B B B B B B B B B

B

Benjamin saw the biggest spider

Benjamin

climbing behind the bench!

climbing

Choose some interesting words from the previous page and write them on the lines below.

Self-assessment   Put a circle around your best letter and word on each page.
Explain your choice to your teacher or classmate.

Tall letter group

3Ps Have you checked your posture, pencil grip and paper position?

Have you done your warm-ups?

key

Trace and then copy the letters and words.

k k k k k k k k k k

k

kicks   kicking   kicked

kicks

know   knows   known

know

kangaroo   koala   kookaburra

kangaroo

k e k l i t o f d o h i b

above
on
below

K K K K K K K K K

K

Keki saw many kangaroos and

Keki

koalas on Kangaroo Island.

koalas

Choose some interesting words from the previous page and write them on the lines below.

Trace the patterns.

Trace and then continue each pattern.

Warm-up patterns for short letters

above

on

below

3Ps Have you checked your posture, pencil grip and paper position?

Have you done your warm-ups?

insect

Trace and then copy the letters and words.

i i i i i i i i i i i

i i i i i i i i i i i

in   if   it   is

i

into   inside   invite

i

invent   invents   invention

i

i a c e o s u v w r m

I imagined that I invented an

incredible robot that could dance.

Choose some interesting words from the previous page and write them on the lines below.

Put a circle around your best letter and word on each page.
Explain your choice to your teacher or classmate.

above
on
below

3Ps Have you checked your posture, pencil grip and paper position?

Have you done your warm-ups?

avocado

Trace and then copy the letters and words.

a a a a a a a a a a a a

a

at   all   are

a

arrive   arrives   arrived

a

ask   asks   asking

a

a c e o s u v w r m n

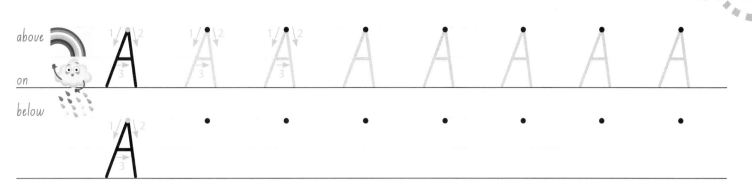

above

on

below

Ali arrived at the Acropolis

A

at exactly the right time today.

Choose some interesting words from the previous page and write them on the lines below.

Put a circle around your best letter and word on each page.
Explain your choice to your teacher or classmate.

3Ps Have you checked your posture, pencil grip and paper position?

Have you done your warm-ups?

car

Trace and then copy the letters and words.

c c c c c c c c c c

c • • • • • • • • •

can   cannot   can't

c

cook   cooking   cooked

c

close   closed   closing

c

c e c o s u v w r m n x

above

on

below

C C C C C C C C

C

Cara cooked a creamy coconut

C

cake for her cousin Chad.

Choose some interesting words from the previous page and write them on the lines below.

Self-assessment Put a circle around your best letter and word on each page. Explain your choice to your teacher or classmate.

Short letter group 29

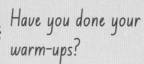

3Ps Have you checked your posture, pencil grip and paper position?

Have you done your warm-ups?

echidna

Trace and then copy the letters and words.

e · · · · · · · · ·

e · · · · · · · · ·

eat   eats   eaten

e

excite   exciting   excited

e

eight   eighteen   eighth

e

e   e   o   s   u   v   w   r   m   n   x   z

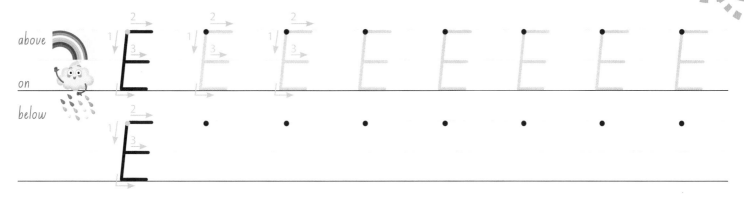

E E E E E E E E E

E

Eddie came eighth in the egg-

E

and-spoon race on sports day.

Choose some interesting words from the previous page and write them on the lines below.

above
on
below

3Ps

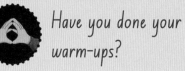
Have you checked your posture, pencil grip and paper position?

Have you done your warm-ups?

octopus

Trace and then copy the letters and words.

o

o

on   off   out   over

o

open   opening   opened

o

order   orders   ordered

o

o   s   u   v   w   r   m   n   x   z   i

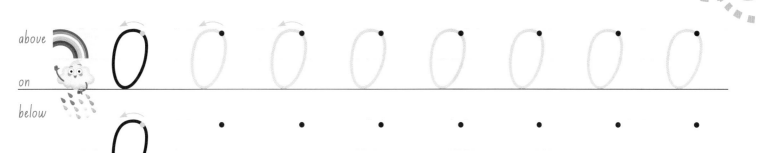

O

O

Olivia and I opened all of our

birthday presents at once!

Choose some interesting words from the previous page and write them on the lines below.

Self-assessment   Put a circle around your best letter and word on each page.
Explain your choice to your teacher or classmate.

OXFORD UNIVERSITY PRESS

Short letter group   33

 3Ps

Have you checked your posture, pencil grip and paper position?

Have you done your warm-ups?

submarine

Trace and then copy the letters and words.

s s s s s s s s s s s s

s · · · · · · · · · · ·

sleep   sleeping   slept

s

silly   sillier   silliest

s

some   someone   something

s

s s u u v v w r m n x z i a

Short letter group

OXFORD UNIVERSITY PRESS

above
on
below

S S S S S S S S S

S

Sami slept in on Monday and

S

was late for school assembly.

Choose some interesting words from the previous page and write them on the lines below.

Self-assessment   Put a circle around your best letter and word on each page. Explain your choice to your teacher or classmate.

3Ps Have you checked your posture, pencil grip and paper position?

Have you done your warm-ups?

umbrella

Trace and then copy the letters and words.

↓u u u u u u u u u u u

↓u • • • • • • • • •

use   uses   using

u

undo   undone   undoing

u

unpack   unpacks   unpacked

u

u v w r m n x z i a c

U U U U U U U U U

U

Uri unpacked his best crayons

U

to draw a picture for his mum.

t

Choose some interesting words from the previous page and write them on the lines below.

Put a circle around your best letter and word on each page.
Explain your choice to your teacher or classmate.

U

3Ps Have you checked your posture, pencil grip and paper position?

Have you done your warm-ups?

vegetables

Trace and then copy the letters and words.

v v v v v v v v v v

v • • • • • • • •

visit   visits   visitors

v

everyone   everybody   everyday

e

vary   varied   various

v

v w r m n x z i a c e

above

on

below

V v v v v v v v v v v v v v v v

V

Vicky and her family saw vultures

v

flying across the wide valley.

f

Choose some interesting words from the previous page and write them on the lines below.

Self-assessment Put a circle around your best letter and word on each page. Explain your choice to your teacher or classmate.

3Ps Have you checked your posture, pencil grip and paper position?

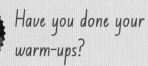

Have you done your warm-ups?

whale

Trace and then copy the letters and words.

w w w w w w w w w w

w • • • • • • • • •

want   wants   wanted

w

walk   walking   walked

w

water   watering   watered

w

w r m n x z i a c e o

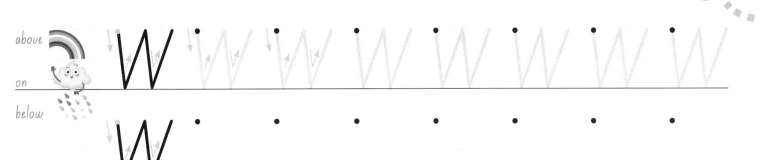

above
on
below

W W W W W W W W W W

W

Willow would have liked to stay

W

for the whole weekend.

I

Choose some interesting words from the previous page and write them on the lines below.

Self-assessment Put a circle around your best letter and word on each page.
Explain your choice to your teacher or classmate.

3Ps Have you checked your posture, pencil grip and paper position?

Have you done your warm-ups?

reading

Trace and then copy the letters and words.

r r r r r r r r r r r

r

run   running   ran

r

rain   rainbow   rainforest

r

refuse   refuses   refused

r

r m n x z i a c e o s

above on below

R R R R R R R R R R

R

Rollo saw a bright rainbow over

R

the lush, tropical rainforest.

Choose some interesting words from the previous page and write them on the lines below.

Put a circle around your best letter and word on each page.
Explain your choice to your teacher or classmate.

above
on
below

3Ps Have you checked your posture, pencil grip and paper position?

Have you done your warm-ups?

mowing

Trace and then copy the letters and words.

m m m m m m m m m m m

m • • • • • • • • •

made   make   making

m

may   monkey   march

m

magic   magical   magically

m

m m x z i a c e o s u

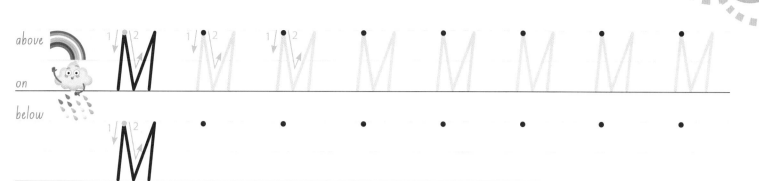

above
on
below

M M M M M M M M M M M M

M

Max and Malia played amazing

M

music at the school concert.

m

Choose some interesting words from the previous page and write them on the lines below.

Self-assessment Put a circle around your best letter and word on each page. Explain your choice to your teacher or classmate.

Short letter group 45

3Ps Have you checked your posture, pencil grip and paper position?

Have you done your warm-ups?

nest

Trace and then copy the letters and words.

n n n n n n n n n n

n · · · · · · · · ·

new   newer   newest

n

nice   nicer   nicest

n

nine   ninth   nineteen

n

n x z i a c e o s u v

above
on
below

N N N N N N N N N N

N

Nick and his family want to see

N

the new film that starts at nine.

t

Choose some interesting words from the previous page and write them on the lines below.

Self-assessment Put a circle around your best letter and word on each page.
Explain your choice to your teacher or classmate.

3Ps Have you checked your posture, pencil grip and paper position?

Have you done your warm-ups?

6

x as in "six"

Trace and then copy the letters and words.

x x x x x x x x x x x

x

box　　fox　　next　　six

b

mix　　fix　　vex　　ox

m

explore　　explores　　explored

e

x z i a c e o s u v w

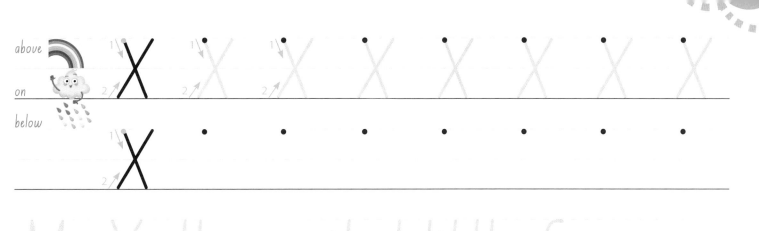

above
on
below

Mr X, the excited little fox,

explored the rabbit hole.

Choose some interesting words from the previous page and write them on the lines below.

Short letter group **49**

above
on
below

z z

3Ps Have you checked your posture, pencil grip and paper position?

Have you done your warm-ups?

zebra

Trace and then copy the letters and words.

z z z z z z z z z z z

z · · · · · · · · · ·

zip   zipper   zigzag

z

lazy   laziest   laziness

l

puzzle   puzzles   puzzled

p

z z a z c e o s u u w r

Z Z Z Z Z Z Z Z

Z

Z

Zahra's popcorn, pizza and puzzle

Z

party was a big hit!

p

Choose some interesting words from the previous page and write them on the lines below.

_____

_____

Teacher comment

Warm-up patterns for tail letters

Trace the patterns.

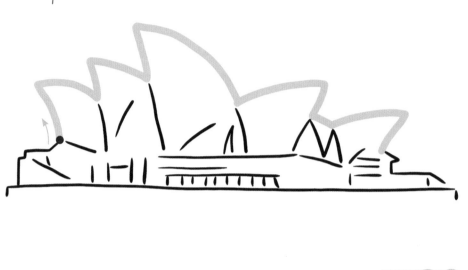

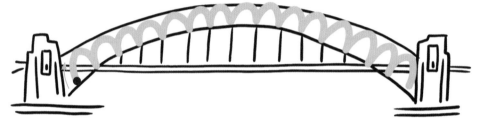

OXFORD UNIVERSITY PRESS

Trace and then continue each pattern.

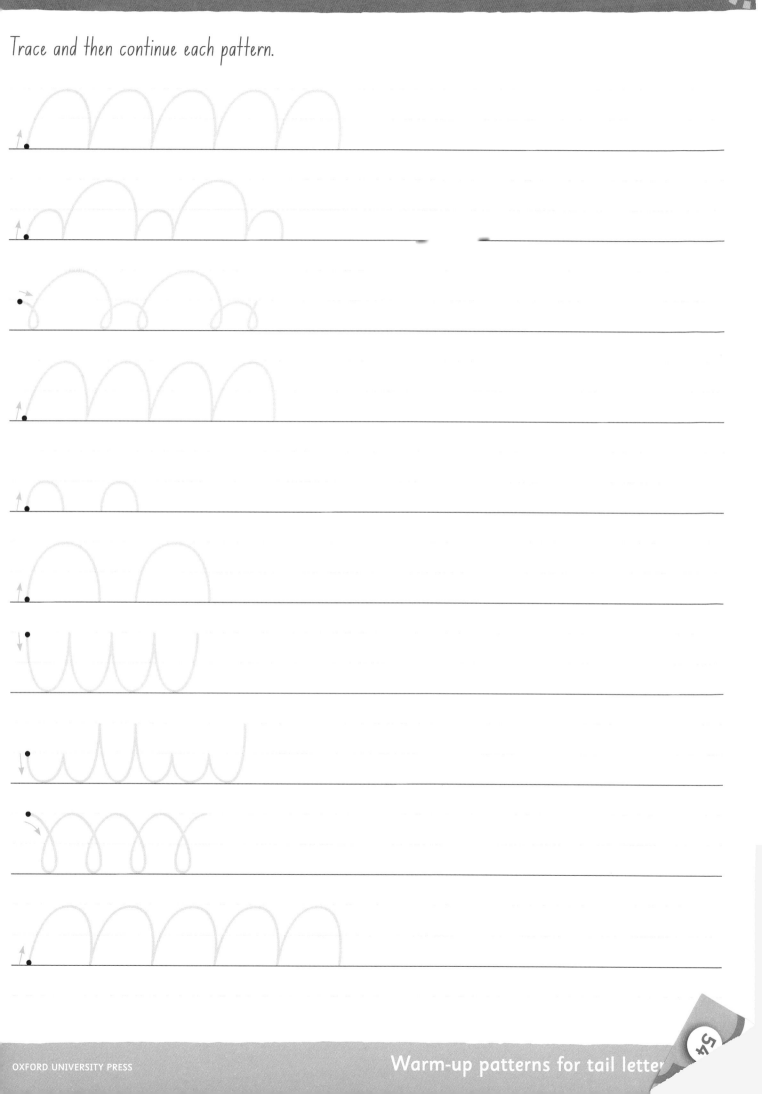

3Ps Have you checked your posture, pencil grip and paper position?

Have you done your warm-ups?

jam

Trace and then copy the letters and words.

joke   joking   joked

jump   jumps   jumping

jungle   justice   judge

j a g e q i y o p u j

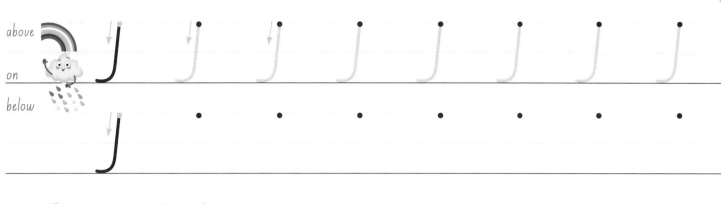

above
on
below

j j j j j j j j j

j

It's just too cold to sit in the

l

plunge pool in June and July.

p

Choose some interesting words from the previous page and write them on the lines below.

Self-assessment

Put a circle around your best letter and word on each page.
Explain your choice to your teacher or classmate.

3Ps Have you checked your posture, pencil grip and paper position?

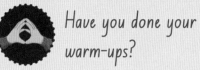 Have you done your warm-ups?

grapes

Trace and then copy the letters and words.

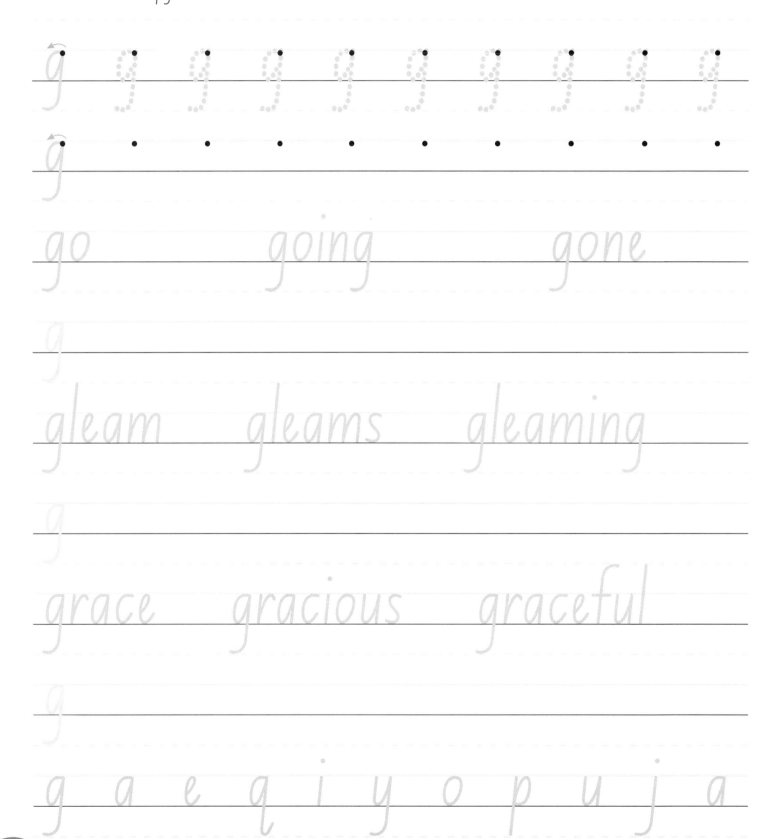

go   going   gone

gleam   gleams   gleaming

grace   gracious   graceful

g a e g i y o p u j a

above
on
below

G G G G G G G G

G

Gino, go and get the green lead.

G

We are going to Gray's paddock.

W

Choose some interesting words from the previous page and write them on the lines below.

Self-assessment Put a circle around your best letter and word on each page.
Explain your choice to your teacher or classmate.

3Ps Have you checked your posture, pencil grip and paper position?

Have you done your warm-ups?

quilt

Trace and then copy the letters and words.

q q q q q q q q q q q

q

quiet   quieter   quietest

q

quick   quicker   quickest

q

quokka   quail   quoll

q

q i y o p u j a g e q

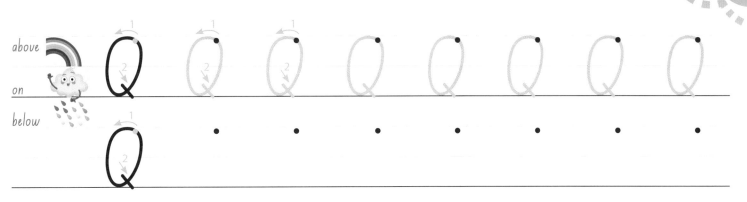

above
on
below

Queenie the quoll moves quickly

Q

and quietly past the quokka.

a

Choose some interesting words from the previous page and write them on the lines below.

Self-assessment
Put a circle around your best letter and word on each page.
Explain your choice to your teacher or classmate.

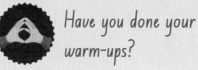

yoga

Trace and then copy the letters and words.

y y y y y y y y y y y

y

you your yours yourself

y

young younger youngest

y

yum yummy yummiest

y

y o p u j a g e q i y

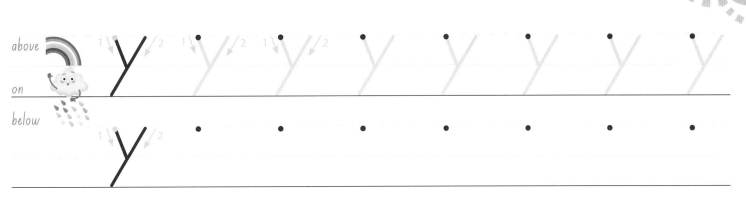

above
on
below

Yesterday, Yindi brought the

y

yummiest lunch to school.

y

Choose some interesting words from the previous page and write them on the lines below.

Self-assessment   Put a circle around your best letter and word on each page.
Explain your choice to your teacher or classmate.

paint

above

on

below

3Ps Have you checked your posture, pencil grip and paper position?

Have you done your warm-ups?

Trace and then copy the letters and words.

p p p p p p p p p p p

p p p p p p p p p p p

play   plays   playing   played

p

pancake   popcorn   pineapple

p

perform   performs   performed

p

p u j a g e q i y o p

OXFORD UNIVERSITY PRESS

above
on
below

P P P P P P P P P

P

Pete's band performed in the

P

playground for the parents.

p

Choose some interesting words from the previous page and write them on the lines below.

Self-assessment   Put a circle around your best letter and word on each page. Explain your choice to your teacher or classmate.

Trace and then copy the lower- and upper-case letters.

aA   bB   cC   dD   eE

fF   gG   hH   iI   jJ   kK

lL   mM   nN   oO   pP

qQ   rR   sS   tT   uU

vV   wW   xX   yY   zZ

Trace the numbers.

1 2 3 4 5 6 7 8 9 10

OXFORD UNIVERSITY PRESS